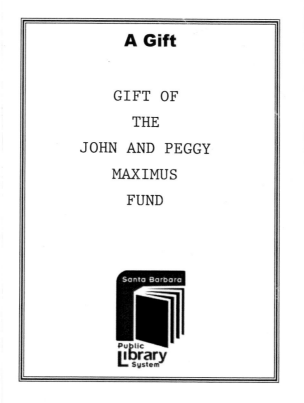

BACKYARD WILDLIFE

Opossums

by Emily Green

BLASTOFF! READERS

BELLWETHER MEDIA • MINNEAPOLIS, MN

Note to Librarians, Teachers, and Parents:

Blastoff! Readers are carefully developed by literacy experts and combine standards-based content with developmentally appropriate text.

Level 1 provides the most support through repetition of high-frequency words, light text, predictable sentence patterns, and strong visual support.

Level 2 offers early readers a bit more challenge through varied simple sentences, increased text load, and less repetition of high-frequency words.

Level 3 advances early-fluent readers toward fluency through increased text and concept load, less reliance on visuals, longer sentences, and more literary language.

Level 4 builds reading stamina by providing more text per page, increased use of punctuation, greater variation in sentence patterns, and increasingly challenging vocabulary.

Level 5 encourages children to move from "learning to read" to "reading to learn" by providing even more text, varied writing styles, and less familiar topics.

Whichever book is right for your reader, Blastoff! Readers are the perfect books to build confidence and encourage a love of reading that will last a lifetime!

This edition first published in 2011 by Bellwether Media, Inc.

No part of this publication may be reproduced in whole or in part without written permission of the publisher. For information regarding permission, write to Bellwether Media, Inc., Attention: Permissions Department, 5357 Penn Avenue South, Minneapolis, MN 55419.

Library of Congress Cataloging-in-Publication Data
Green, Emily K., 1966-
  Opossums / by Emily Green.
      p. cm. – (Backyard wildlife)
  Includes bibliographical references and index.
  Summary: "Developed by literacy experts for students in kindergarten through grade three, this book introduces opossums to young readers through leveled text and related photos"–Provided by publisher.
  ISBN 978-1-60014-561-2 (hardcover : alk. paper)
  1. Opossums–Juvenile literature. I. Title.
  QL737.M34G74 2011
  599.2'76–dc22   2010034532

Printed in the United States of America, North Mankato, MN.

010111   1176

Contents

Opossums are **marsupials** with white and black fur. They do not have fur on their ears, feet, or tails.

Opossums live
in grasslands,
forests, and
cities. They like
to live by water.

Opossums are good climbers. Sharp **claws** on their feet help them grip branches.

Opossums use their long tails to hold on to branches. This helps them keep their **balance**.

Opossums eat
plants, fruits,
insects, and mice.
They also eat
eggs and snails.

Opossums need
to stay safe
from **predators**.
They look for
food at night
and hide during
the day.

Sometimes an opossum meets a predator. It shows its 50 teeth to scare the predator away.

A female opossum
has a **pouch**
on her belly.
She carries her
new babies in it.

Baby opossums live
in the pouch for
six to eight weeks.
Then they come out.
Hello opossums!

Glossary

balance—to stay steady and not fall

claws—sharp, curved nails on the feet of opossums; claws help opossums climb.

insects—small animals with six legs and hard outer bodies; insect bodies are divided into three parts.

marsupials—animals that carry their young in a pouch attached to the belly

pouch—a pocket of skin on the belly of a female marsupial; a marsupial uses its pouch to carry its young.

predators—animals that hunt other animals for food

To Learn More

AT THE LIBRARY

Bogue, Gary. *There's an Opossum in My Backyard*. Berkeley, Calif.: Heyday Books, 2007.

Jacobs, Lee. *Opossum*. San Diego, Calif.: Blackbirch Press, 2003.

Macken, JoAnn Early. *Opossums*. Pleasantville, N.Y.: Weekly Reader Pub., 2010.

ON THE WEB

Learning more about opossums is as easy as 1, 2, 3.

1. Go to www.factsurfer.com.

2. Enter "opossums" into the search box.

3. Click the "Surf" button and you will see a list of related Web sites.

With factsurfer.com, finding more information is just a click away.

Index

The images in this book are reproduced through the courtesy of: Phillip W. Kirkland, front cover; Gordon & Cathy Illg/Animals Animals – Earth Scenes, pp. 5, 11; Rick & Nora Bowers/Alamy, pp. 7, 9, 21; WDG Photo, p. 7 (left); Juan Martinez, pp. 7 (middle), 13 (right); S. Borisov, p. 7 (right); Jack Milchanowski/Photolibrary, p. 13; Ew Chee Guan, p. 13 (left); Eduard Kyslynskyy, p. 13 (middle); Rolf Nussbaumer/Photolibrary, p. 15; Rex Lisman, p. 17; S.J. Krasemann/Photolibrary, p. 19.